THE SAINT AUGUSTINE LECTURE SERIES
Villanova University

Saint Augustine and

the Augustinian Tradition

Robert P. Russell, O.S.A.
ASSOCIATE EDITOR

Robert P. Russell, O.S.A.
EDITOR

Benedict A. Paparella, Ph.D.
ASSOCIATE EDITOR

THE SAINT AUGUSTINE LECTURE 1965

THE RESURRECTION
AND SAINT AUGUSTINE'S
THEOLOGY OF HUMAN VALUES

HENRI IRÉNÉE MARROU

Translated from the French by
Mother Maria Consolata, S.H.C.J.

Nihil obstat: Joseph Quigley, J.C.D.
    Censor Librorum

Imprimatur: +John J. Krol
Archbishop of Philadelphia

January 14, 1966

Library of Congress catalog card number: 66-30457

INTRODUCTION

Except for the addition of a substantial number of notes, this short work reproduces in English translation the Saint Augustine Lecture given at Villanova University in the Fall of 1964. It comprises the seventh in a series of annual Lectures introduced at Villanova University in 1959, having for the general subject "Saint Augustine and the Augustinian Tradition." Prompted by the conviction that Augustine's teachings are both timeless and timely, the University invites each year an outstanding scholar to present some facet of the Saint's vast range of thought particularly relevant to the problems of contemporary man and society.

Professor Marrou is widely known for his many valuable contributions in the fields of classical, patristic, and historical research. In the present work, "The Resurrection and Saint Augustine's Theology of Human Values," the author offers a brilliant and richly documented account of the Saint's theology of human values. His conclusions should go far towards placing in true perspective an aspect of Augustine that has failed to receive the attention it deserves.

The Editor wishes to express his gratitude to Mother Mary Consolata, S.H.C.J., of Rosemont College, who generously undertook the task of translating the manuscript from French into English.

Robert P. Russell, O.S.A., Editor

Villanova University

Villanova, Pennsylvania

The Resurrection
and Saint Augustine's
Theology of Human Values

The Resurrection and Saint Augustine's Theology of Human Values

Saint Augustine has often been charged with a kind of contempt for specifically human values and for those subordinated goals of human conduct which obviously occupy a secondary place. This reproach has been formulated especially in placing St. Augustine's theology in opposition to that of St. Thomas, where the latter is said to be more open to such values, more explicit, or more complete, or at least, better balanced. It is a completely unwarranted over-simplification to summarize the whole development of theological thought by reducing it to an opposition of two rival or complementary currents, Augustinianism and Thomism, Neoplatonic and Aristotelian respectively. Although antithesis is a convenient figure of rhetoric which can be useful to theology, as St. Augustine's own example has shown—and St. Paul's before him—it should not be abused. As I have written elsewhere, the whole complex richness of historical experience cannot be adequately modulated by a two-holed flute.[1] The fact that St. Augustine and St. Thomas ought not to be set too systematically in opposition has been magnificently exemplified by the theological tradition of the Order of the Hermits of St. Augustine, a tradition rendered illustrious by so many eminent doctors, beginning with Giles of Rome.

To return to the problem of human values: it is

certainly true that in the thought and above all in the spirituality of St. Augustine there is an impatience, as it were, an urgency to mount, and to leave behind the lower rungs in the hierarchy of beings, to neglect secondary causes and subordinate ends, and to press forward as directly as possible towards Him who is both First Cause and Highest Good—Cause of all that is, and Final End which fills to overflowing all need, all aspiration, all expectation. Let us recall here the deeply moving words of that great prayer which we read at the opening of the *Soliloquies,*[2] a prayer which St. Augustine wrote just after his conversion and which expresses some of the sentiments, as well as the deep tendency characteristic of his religious temperament. This Augustinian spirituality can well be defined by the verse of St. Matthew's Gospel: "Seek first the kingdom of God and His justice, and all these things"—that is, all these poor humble human values—"will be given you besides," *et haec omnia adjicientur vobis* . . . .[3] In one sense, the whole essence of Augustinianism is contained in the *porro unum necessarium* of *Luke* X, 42, in the pericope of Martha and Mary, on which the Saint composed a number of beautiful sermons.[4]

Yet it is dangerous to attempt to reduce a whole body of thought, an entire theology, to a slogan or a word. Augustinianism is, admittedly, that *unum est necessarium*, but it is much more as well, and happily so. It would be very serious if a Christian mind as rich and as authentic as St. Augustine's, in whom the Church has always recognized one of her greatest teachers (less than a year after his death, Pope St. Celestine I so styled him *inter magistros optimos*[5]), could have been completely unaware of, or have excluded from his doctrinal synthesis this problem of the justification of human values—a problem which today so sharply challenges Christian thought. For the Christian today is rightly eager to engage in dialogue with the world in which he has been placed (if we may use the same words which Pope Paul VI employed with such emphasis in his first encyclical, *Ecclesiam suam*). And the dialogue is with modern civilization, which is so proud, overproud perhaps, of its accomplishments in the temporal order.

It would, I say, be serious. Fortunately, there is no question of this. I shall try to demonstrate this fact by choosing from among many other themes (for many others could be cited) the dogma of the resurrection of the body. This choice can be justified for many reasons. First of all, as we shall see, it is an area in which St. Augustine consciously opposed the Neoplatonism of his pagan masters. (Augustinian Platonism, like every other Christian philosophy, introduces the necessary clarifications and corrections where pagan thought had erred for lack of guidance or support by revelation. St. Thomas was to do the same with reference to Aristotle.) It is therefore a point at which we are sure to lay hold of a thought that is both really and deeply personal.

Secondly, St. Augustine had reason to return to this doctrine and to speak about it throughout his long ecclesiastical career. He treats it emphatically in *De fide et symbolo* which, as a young priest, he had the honor of preaching on October 8, 393,[6] before a council of the African bishops assembled at Hippo. He discusses it again in reply to an objection made by his indefatigable opponent Julian of Eclanum in the *Opus imperfectum* on which he was working when death overtook him.[7] The doctrine of the resurrection holds an important place in his presentations of theological syntheses, whether they be brief and destined for the use of the faithful, like the *Enchiridion ad Laurentium,*[8] or fully developed and directed against the pagans, as the *City of God*, which devotes to this matter long chapters of Book XIII (on the subject of death) or Book XX (on judgment), as well as the greater part of the last book, Book XXII.

Why so prominent a place? Primarily, because the doctrine of the final resurrection is one of the fundamental dogmas of the Christian faith. The Creed, or, as St. Augustine more often says, the *confessio fidei,*[9] devotes an article to it. It is noteworthy that this article is not missing from any one of the ancient versions which have come down to us, except perhaps, and by chance, in the later *Canons* of Hippolytus— but this last point is contested. The form which the catechumens of Hippo learned in preparation for baptism begins *Credo in Deum Patrem* and continues toward the end: *in sanctam Ecclesiam, remissionem peccatorum et resurrectionem carnis.* The unending discussions about the African or Augustinian (Mila-

4

nese?) text of this creed do not bear on the article in question here, an article which is attested by every one of the sources since Tertullian.

It is precisely this place of honor given to an essential element of faith which explains the role played by the resurrection of the body in what we would today call Augustine's pastoral teaching, i.e., the ordinary teaching of the bishop of Hippo in his episcopal capacity: *precatechesis* or first presentation of Christianity to pagans of good will, the *accedentes,* an instruction for which *De catechizandis rudibus* supplies us with both theory and model;[10] catechesis properly so called, in the sermons preparing for baptism:[11] the *traditio symboli*, and hence its commentary were an important episode in this preparation. The discipline of the secret[12] required that the text of the *Credo* be not handed down in writing; therefore, on a specified day it was made known to those about to be baptized, the *competentes*, who were given a week to learn it by heart and who recited it a week later, *redditio symboli*. The exact date of these ceremonies has not yet been determined. We know a good deal about the liturgical year at Hippo, but not as much as we would like to. However, some pieces of evidence assign the *traditio symboli* to the Tuesday after Palm Sunday.[13] Finally, not to mention the various occasions which might occur now and then during the annual cycle of preaching, such as the feast of the Dedication[14] or a commentary on *Ps.* 29, 3: *Domine eduxisti ab inferno animam meam,*[15] the same theme appears regularly in a third type of sermon: sermons for Easter week, wherein Christ's resurrection, the very core of Christian faith,[16] rightly occupies the place of honor.[17] St. Augustine tells us that this primordial resurrection appears as the first fruits and pledge, *exemplum*,[18] of that promised to us and the two are inseparable, as is so fittingly emphasized by St. Paul in Chapter XV (v. 12) of *First Corinthians*: "Now if Christ is preached as risen from the dead, how do some among you say that there is no resurrection of the dead?" St. Augustine never tires of referring to this text either explicitly or implicitly in almost every passage which he devotes to this subject.[19]

Nor is this all. In addition to being shepherd of souls, he is doctor-theologian, which in the fourth and fifth centuries was equivalent to controversialist. St. Augustine was led to plumb the dogma of the resurrection in order to meet objections which heretics on all sides were raising against it: Gnostics, represented at that time by the Manicheans[20] and the pagans. These objections were nothing new. Witness the discourse on the Areopagus as reported in the *Acts of the Apostles,* chapter XVII. St. Paul had no more than pronounced the words "risen from the dead" with reference to Christ when his hearers— Stoic and Epicurean philosophers alike—interrupted him and covered him with ridicule (v.33). Things had not changed much in St. Augustine's time. The notion of resurrection was the great problem encountered in the evangelization of the ancient world. It was a stumbling block for the mind of the time, offending the sentiment of the masses as well as the reflection of the learned. It is surprising to see the considerable number of objections which for a long time were raised against it. In a study which has since remained a classic, "Propos antichrétiens rapportés par saint Augustin," Pierre Courcelle has catalogued more than a dozen pertaining to this point,[21] and the list could be extended. It is noteworthy that some among them, stated in the very same words, had already been discussed in the latter half of the second century by the early apologists,[22] Athenagoras of Athens (c.177) or Tertullian (197 and after). It seems that they were still circulating with such persistence that St. Augustine took care to answer them, even in his most informal preaching.[23]

Many of these objections seem to us today either captious or naive. For example, what was the destiny of the foetus lost by abortion? And, concerning children, what size clothing would they wear? And what of physical defects? Would some of the risen be obese, some emaciated, some even deformed? And what about hair and nails which had been clipped during a person's lifetime? And suppose the dust to which corpses were reduced had been dispersed by the wind, or carried away by floods? The fate of the drowned seemed especially disturbing—particularly those devoured by sharks. And finally, the greatest difficulty of all, how would those poor victims arise who had been eaten and assimilated by cannibals? Among the learned, objections were more philosophical. If, for instance, every element—earth, water, air, fire—had the place in the universe which its weight determined, how could our body, terrestrial as it is, be lifted up to heaven?[24] This was an old objection which Cicero had long ago formulated against the apotheosis of Romulus[25] and to which Eusebius had given status in his apology against Heraclitus. Its reasoning is on a par with that of Soviet propaganda against God, emphasizing that the astronauts did not come across God in outer space—as if when we spoke of heaven we meant the material space of the physicists!

To each of these objections St. Augustine was obliged to answer as best he could—with considerable ingenuity sometimes—as he did in the case of cannibalism, to cite but a single example. He opined that the flesh under discussion belonged personally to the victim and that the cannibal, having merely borrowed it, would have to return it on the day of resurrection to its original owner![26] Another example could be instanced in the comparison wherein a sculptor melts down and then remakes a metal statue without bothering to see if each particle of metal returns to the same place which it had originally occupied.[27] The same metaphor occurs in a different context in the writing of St. John Chrysostom: we need not lament that our body must be destroyed before rising again —no one grieves about founding metal in order to remake it into a statue . . . .[28]

This is not dogmatic theology, but only apologetics which must, like Penelope, work out an answer to every objection against the faith. "Be ready always with an answer," exhorts the *First Epistle of St. Peter,* "to everyone who asks a reason for the hope that is in you" (3,15). We must not linger over this superficial imagery, but rather consider the deep roots of such strong opposition to the dogma of the resurrection. If there was anything that could pass as solidly established and definitively elucidated in the eyes of ancient thought—and this is above all true for the contemporaries of St. Augustine, when the dominant mode of thought or *Zeitgeist* was more or less completely molded by Neoplatonism—that something was a certain metaphysical disqualification of the body and of everything in us which, because of the body, was dependent on crude matter. We shall shortly see St. Augustine engage in controversy with Porphyry. How characteristic it is to note that the latter can find nothing more praiseworthy to say of his master Plotinus—it is the very first sentence of his biography of the master—"Plotinus seemed to feel ashamed of dwelling in a body."[29] To the eyes of the pagan philosopher the body appeared as a prison for the soul, a tomb. (The Platonic *soma-sama* had become famous.) St. Augustine was familiar with this theme, having met it, for instance, in Vergil,[30] and he had written against it more than once.[31] The whole aim of the moralist tended to struggle against the body, to master or even destroy fleshly passions. At this point even Epicurean materialism rejoined the ascetical ideal of the other schools. What a paradox therefore to talk of a resurrection of the body! It is quite remarkable that even though the word *anastasis* occurs once in Plotinus' writings (of course in the literal sense of a "spiritual raising up" and not of "resurrection"), it does so in a passage directed against those who are overly concerned with the body. The barb is aimed at the Stoics. They are said to be like dreamers, who mistake for reality what they have seen in sleep, saying that everything which has to do with the body must be considered unreal; that in order not to be led astray by false appearances one must effect a raising up through separation from the body (*anastasis apo tou sômatos*); that merely passing from one body to another would amount to about the same as having an invalid change beds.[32]

As with moral, so with speculative action, everything led to differentiating from the body and demonstrating the superiority of a higher element—soul, spirit, *hègemonikon,* the name matters little—by which man participated in the divine nature. Witness Plotinus' last words uttered on his death bed as the same Porphyry recounts them: "I am trying to uplift what is divine in us to the divine in the universe."[33] These philosophers held that man had, or to speak more exactly, that man *was* a spark of divinity, a part of the substance of God, temporarily and very regrettably imprisoned in flesh, from which it could only long to be set free. The Gnostics were in accord here with the Platonists: to know, to recognize this fundamental condition was in their eyes the essence of the Gnosis, that esoteric knowledge which they claimed to possess by a secret revelation and to reveal in turn to those whom they initiated in it.

It is well known that Gnosticism, a very different religion from Christianity, was led for strategic and propagandistic reasons to assume a Christian mask. The Gnostics could not thereafter avoid using the word "resurrection" themselves, a word which, as we have seen, was such an essential component of the Christian message. Yet, though they preserved the borrowed term *anastasis,* they used it only in a figurative sense which emptied it of its real meaning. This is clearly proved by the recently published treatise *De resurrectione* which was found among the manuscripts of Nag-Hammadi.[34] Just as in Plotinus, what is here meant is a spiritual uplifting, brought about by conscious attention to this basic truth revealed by secret tradition. For them, as well as for the mysterious heretics assailed in the Second Epistle to Timothy (2.18),[35] who were perhaps Gnostics *avant la lettre*, at the moment the Gnostic—that higher and 'pneumatic' being—became aware of his true nature, then, for him "the resurrection has already taken place." Philosophers and Gnostics were at one in opposing this fundamental article of Christian faith. St. Augustine would have to engage in controversy on this same point against the Manicheans and the Neoplatonist pagans.

In this insistence on preaching the resurrection of the body, in season and out of season, the ancients could see only an obsession, a paradox pushed to the limits of the absurd. What! After having struggled so long against the body and its unhappy tendencies, was man to join once again that wretched partner, that old rag—and for all eternity? A cultured pagan like Celsus, the first philosopher to undertake a systematic refutation of Christianity (as early as the end of the second century), just could not understand how anyone could cherish such a hope. As he saw it, this was proof that Christians were ignoramuses, barbarians—by which he meant primitives whose ethnological mental processes were below the level of reason. He could find only one way to explain this preoccupation which seemed to him so extraordinary: that in their undeveloped state and their naive ignorance, Christians could not grasp any other than sensible knowledge and believed that in order to see God they needed eyes of flesh![36] St. Augustine, whether in his learned treatises such as *The City of God*[37] or in his sermons addressed to the unlettered faithful,[38] would never weary of returning to, and refuting, the categorical formula in which Porphyry summed up his position. Whether this was in *De regressu animae* or, as my friend John J. O'Meara has tried to establish, in the *Philosophy of the Oracles,*[39] matters little. It was a proposition so essential to Neoplatonism and to ancient thought that Porphyry must not have been the only one to formulate it: *Corpus omne est fugiendum,* "we must get free of whatever, either within us or outside us, has to do with the body."

There is no longer question here of objections, more or less amusing, about sharks and cannibals. This is a metaphysical problem, and a most serious one at that. We have reached a decisive alternative.

12

Either there is in man something divine, in the strictest sense of the word, (and this could only be the most spiritual part of him, for it would be blasphemous to associate with it the body which, from this point on, becomes a discredit and even an enemy) or else man is a creature, capable indeed of receiving what the Greek Fathers boldly call divinization[40] and which remains a created reality. We must add immediately, in order to confront the pessimism of the Gnostics, that this creature is the work, not of an ignorant or evil demiurge, but of a God who is as utterly good as He is all-powerful.[41] Hence it follows (and St. Augustine obstinately repeats to his former Manichean friends) that everything this God has graciously willed to create is also good—in its own order of course, and at its own level of being: And God saw that it was good. This versicle, as we all know, recurs as a refrain in the account of creation given in *Genesis*.[42]

In this entirely different perspective the resurrection of the body ceases to be a stumbling block. Moreover, the Christian faith presents it as the second part of a diptych: to creation there corresponds the Incarnation. The "flesh" is so far from being despicable that the Word of God willed to assume it. The Gnostics, consistently enough, were usually Docetists: the Saviour who was manifested in Jesus of Nazareth could not have anything more than the appearance of a body, or a borrowed body. The Incarnation, taken in the full sense in which orthodox faith receives it—Jesus Christ, true God and true man—

13

entails consequences which bear on the present problem. Reversing the adage so often used against the Appolinarists,[43] it could be said that everything which has been assumed must in some manner be saved. Redemption extends to our body also, as St. Augustine emphasizes in the very words of St. Paul (*Romans* 8, 23): *certa spe adoptionem exspectamus, redemptionem corporis nostri.*[44]

These considerations lead the Christian thinker to a totally different anthropology from that of pagan philosophy. Man is no longer to be defined solely or even primarily in terms of the spiritual part of him, but is seen as a composite of soul and body (if I may be permitted for brevity's sake to borrow the terminology of classical theology).[45] Moreover—and this is an important point—it is not to the body but to the soul that we must attribute the origin of sin, of evil, of corruption within us.[46]

Here I must make a semantic digression. We know that interpretation of St. Augustine's thought is rendered especially delicate by the fact that the bishop of Hippo, whether speaking as philosopher or as theologian, never ceases to be a great writer, a classicist, respectful of the usage of the triple tradition whose heir he was in the use of the three manners of speech: literary, biblical, and ecclesiastical. He does not confine himself to a technical vocabulary, using each term in a rigorously univocal sense. For instance, it has sometimes been attempted to establish, if not a distinction, at least shades of difference between the terms "resurrection of the dead," "of the body," "of the flesh," but St. Augustine uses the three formulae within a few pages or a few lines of each other with apparently no other concern than to vary the expression.[47]

So it is with regard to the human composite. Take for example the earliest of the relevant texts, the *De fide et symbolo*. Augustine's rich and supple language reflects, now philosophical tradition (whether general, or specific to each school), now biblical usage (which itself varies so greatly). The word *flesh* is sometimes pejorative: "the flesh lusts against the spirit;" sometimes designates man in his totality: "the Word was made flesh." The two currents, philosophical and biblical, sometimes unite. The use of the word *mens*, by which St. Augustine likes to designate the highest point of the human soul submissive to God by faith and the exercise of good will, is undoubtedly influenced by the usage of *bona mens*, an expression made classical by Seneca, as well as by the words of the Apostle (*Romans* 7, 25): "I myself with my mind serve the law of God" (*mente servio legi Dei*). The meaning assigned these words, and their selection, varies according to changing points of view, ontological or moral, without of course destroying the coherence of the thought. Correspondences among these parallel analyses can be established as in the following table.[48]

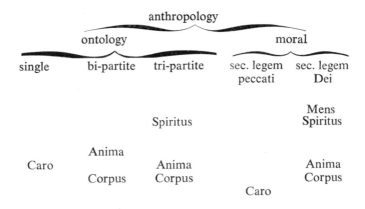

	anthropology			
	ontology		moral	
single	bi-partite	tri-partite	sec. legem peccati	sec. legem Dei
				Mens Spiritus
		Spiritus		
	Anima			
Caro		Anima		Anima
	Corpus	Corpus		Corpus
			Caro	

Through all these variations of vocabulary and viewpoint St. Augustine tries to express a single fundamental truth: man is at one and the same time soul *and* body, flesh *and* spirit; and if man is to be truly saved his salvation must embrace his whole being, and therefore the body must also, by glorious resurrection, be taken up into eternity. We cannot attempt within the limits of this lecture to follow St. Augustine's teaching on this subject in all its ramifications. It will suffice here to reduce it to its essentials with reference to the specific and quite limited end which we have proposed: the theology of human values.

It is striking what prudence and circumspection mark every one of St. Augustine's remarks concerning the fate which awaits us after the resurrection—a subject all the more difficult for its being outside our daily experience. He never misses an opportunity of stressing either our ignorance[49] or the hypothetical nature of the solutions which he suggests.[50] If, for example, he risks speculating on the agility of glorified bodies,[51] we note that his hypothesis is deduced from a scriptural verse (that of *Wisdom* 9, 15): "for the corruptible body burdens the soul and the earthen shelter weighs down the mind that has many concerns." St. Augustine's theology, like that of the Fathers, always rests directly on Holy Scripture. He usually prefers to limit himself to what it explicitly reveals, and primarily to what the Gospels tell us about the risen Christ.

He returns frequently to this point, namely, that the resurrection of the body is really not entirely an object of future hope. The paschal mystery, the resurrection of Christ, is also an accomplished fact, an event, which faith accepts as historical, the heart and the vital center of all Christian faith.[52] Time in the Church, inaugurated by this event, is messianic time. We are living under the reign of eschatology already begun, inchoate. St. Augustine constantly recalls this fundamental point: Christ's resurrection is the exemplary type, the first fruits of our own; and Augustine uses the occasion to develop his theology of the *Christus totus*, or as we say today, of the Mystical Body. Let us listen to him as he gives his catechumens a commentary on the creed:

> We also believe in the resurection of the body which has first come out of Christ, so that the Body also may hope for what has already been done for the Head. The Head of the Church is Christ; the Church is the

body of Christ. Our Head is risen and has ascended into heaven. Where the Head is, there also the members will be.[53]

Our body will become like the body of Christ as it was when He appeared to the disciples from Easter morning to the day of His ascension.[54] This is of course the doctrinal schema which had supported St. Paul's argument in the important text of Chapter 15 of the *First Epistle to the Corinthians,* to which, as we have seen, St. Augustine constantly referred —notably to v.20: "But as it is, Christ is risen from the dead, the first fruits of those who have fallen asleep . . . ."

St. Augustine drew his entire theology of the resurrection from this chapter, supplemented by some further passages from the New Testament, e.g. *Luke* 21,18: "Not a hair of your head shall perish."[55] The account of the transfiguration, *Matthew* 17, 1-8, and parallel passages allowed him to perpetuate the classical metaphor of the body as garment of the soul. On the other hand, the body also will be made resplendent in glory, will put on immortality.[56] And finally, the text to which St. Augustine holds especially (because he finds there the most explicit teaching on what will be the status of the glorified body), the pericope of the woman who had wed successively the seven brothers (*Matthew* 22, 23-33 and parallel passages): ". . . . at the resurrection, truly, they will neither marry nor be given in marriage, but will be as angels of God in heaven."[57]

18

This reference was especially valuable to Augustine in allowing him, while attaching the highest possible value to the bodily resurrection, to free it from all crude materialism. Always following closely the teaching of St. Paul (and above all I *Corinthians* 15, 42-51), St. Augustine emphasizes the profound transformation which our bodies will undergo in the very act of resurrection, passing from the physical to the spiritual, from earthly to celestial. Such equivalent words as *mutatio, commutatio, immutatio, caelestis* or *angelica* (the reference to *Matthew* 22,30 is apparent here) come often from his pen.[58]

And yet, despite such a change, it will indeed always remain the same body, our same body. St. Augustine was unfailingly explicit on this point, which is indeed essential. In the year 426 he even rectified in his *Retractions* an expression on this point deemed ambiguous in his *De agone christiano*, a minor popularizing work written thirty years earlier.[59] The decisive argument here again is the example of the risen Christ. As St. Augustine explains to his correspondent Consentius, referring to St. Luke's account (24,29): "See my hands and feet, that it is I myself," the body of Jesus, now spiritualized, risen as a conqueror from the tomb, is indeed the same body, perfectly recognizable, the same in everything except that it is henceforth freed from corruption, *absumens omnem corruptionem.*[60] The "change," the *immutatio* (the word, just as the whole of the vocabulary which Augustine uses in treating of this question is taken directly from St. Paul, I. *Cor.* 15,52) consists in freeing the body

19

from all the disastrous consequences of sin, of evil, of mortality, in such a way as to confer upon it what St. Paul calls *aphtharsia*, a term rather awkwardly rendered by *incorruptio* in the Latin of St. Augustine, who was faithful, as always, to the *usus ecclesiasticus* —which, unfortunately means here the impoverished vocabulary of the first Latin translators of the Bible. (Our modern translators, enriched by scholastic technicality, render the word *"incorruptibility."*)

St. Augustine makes constant reference to this point and invariably refers to St. Paul's words: ". . . and the dead shall rise incorruptible and we shall be changed. For this incorruptible body must put on incorruption, and this mortal being must put on immortality" (I *Cor.* 15, 52-53). [61] We should not fail to emphasize the immense metaphysical implication of such a stand. Since the time of Aristotle it had been accepted that whatever was introduced into being by becoming (*genesis*), was by the very fact subject to corruption (*phthora*). By forcing us to dissociate the two ideas, faith in the resurrection destroys this too narrow conception within which ancient thought had until then remained imprisoned.

We can see at once how far-reaching are the consequences. The flight from the body, the *omne corpus fugiendum* of Porphyry, no longer appears as the highest ideal to be held up to the soul enamoured of perfection; and St. Augustine comments, with that minute detail dear to all the Fathers since Origen, on the verse of *Wisdom* 9, 15: "the corruptible body burdens the soul." Scripture says specifically "corruptible" to show that it is not the body *qua* body which weighs down the soul, but the state of the body to which it was reduced by sin.[62] On the contrary, we must recognize that the soul was made for the body and that, separated from it, she aspires to rejoin it, and lives in this hope[63]—provided that it be henceforth freed from corruption. The better to persuade the pagans against whom he is writing, St. Augustine tries to wrest from the Platonic myths themselves an acknowledgement of such an ideal: are not the gods of the *Timaeus* defined as souls associated with incorruptible bodies, and that for eternity?[64]

The resurrection will bring about the disappearance of whatever has affected the body or wounded the integrity of its substance;[65] it is a restitution, a *restitutio—in melius*, St. Augustine hastens to specify.[66] (G. B. Ladner very well saw in his excellent book on the notion of reform, that according to Christian theology, history is not cyclic but opens out into a better state.) This idea, which first appears in Tertullian, receives particular stress in the Latin Fathers:[67] the body must be returned to its true nature,[68] to that which constitutes its proper reality. This, too, is from St. Paul, though it comes this time from the *Epistle to the Romans* (8,21: "creation itself will also be delivered from its slavery to corruption . . .," etc.).

In order to express this process, St. Augustine even used the comparison of circumcision.[69] However, we should not force the metaphor, for we must not represent the procedure as a subtraction. The *corruptio* is not a further entity superadded to the properties of the body. Since it is an evil, it is a diminution, a degradation, a further gap introduced into the substance, already lacunary, of the created being. This notion of *corruptio* cannot be understood except in relationship with the fundamental doctrine of the non-substantive nature of evil.[70] This great truth received such refinement of analysis and such brilliance from the pen of our Saint that one is tempted to consider it as specifically his. (It was through having rediscovered it that he had been able to get free of the pessimistic dualism that had detained him so long among the Manicheans.) Yet we must recognize it as a Christian truth common to all the great representatives of the theological tradition, as can be seen as far back as Origen; and even he had predecessors.[71]

The resurrection is therefore a fuller, a better state, incomparably superior to anything we can have known or experienced during our earthly life. Nevertheless, it will be in the same order of reality, although thenceforth possessed of a spiritual quality, our body will yet remain forever our very same body.

And by the same token (for the moment has finally come to take cognizance of it) all those values on the strictly human level will be saved, being raised up together with the body for all eternity, *in vitam aeternam*, as the Creed clearly states in this connection. Once having entered, together with the body, into the realm of the eternal and immutable, they will be freed from all corruption. We know how highly St.

Augustine esteemed immutability, the highest attribute of divinity, the magnificent gift which God reserves for His elect. Nothing is more characteristic of the sensitivity of St. Augustine than the suffering with regard to the instability of our terrestrial state, which is conditioned and summarized by the very fact of our being placed in a temporal order—time, that destroyer of being, wherein our life is consumed and hastens towards death. "There is no one who will not be closer to death a year from now than at this moment, and tomorrow than today, who is not closer today than yesterday. The span of time which one has lived is that much cut off from what remains to be lived, and what remains of it grows less every day; so that all the time of this life is no more than a race towards death . . . ."[72]

In vitam aeternam: fixed thenceforth in a state of permanence,[73] man will once more find, but in their fulness and, as it were, developed to their full potential, all the riches with which God had dowered him as a creature, all those values which earthly life, at least ephemerally and partially, permitted him to taste: the body itself, first of all, and its beauty.[74] For to anyone who has not had long contact with the richness of St. Augustine's work, and who knows him only by an image, so stereotyped as to amount to caricature, which the schools have made traditional, it always comes as a surprise to discover with what praise the great African doctor honors corporeal beauty. And he did not do this necessarily because of the demands of controversy, or because he would not yield to the Manicheans on the abandonment of the flesh to the realms of darkness because of its material nature, or to mock Porphyry, who was vainly determined to flee everything corporeal. It was as a great artist that Augustine spoke, a man concerning whom we know (because he openly avowed it in such vibrant words) was quite sensitive to all the aspects of corporeal beauty. It is not necessary to re-read the *Confessions* in order to realize this; it suffices to listen to the bishop of Hippo preaching quite simply to his people: "If even now so much bodily beauty is seen in our flesh, *tanta corporis pulchritudo*, how much greater will it be there, *ibi* (the *nunc* is opposed almost technically to the eschatological *ibi*).[75] Unfortunately time does not permit us to translate and comment fully upon the beautiful passage of Sermon 243 *in toto*![76] When he thus celebrates the magnificent harmony which reigns in the human body, St. Augustine readily associates with the visible beauty the secret combinations which govern the whole interior architecture of the organism which, as a good Pythagorean (the Platonic tradition had gathered in and integrated the whole legacy of Pythagoras), he calls the *numeri*, and which we may term relationships capable of being analyzed mathematically.[77] If he could have known the remarkable development of our nuclear physics (what is matter for the modern scientist but a system of equations?) there is no doubt that St. Augustine would have welcomed with joy as a superb illustration of his thesis what science teaches today on the geometrically complex structure of our macromolecules and the links which are spaced along

24

the spirals of deoxyribonucleic acid. St. Augustine thought that after the resurrection all that secret harmony would be laid open, and that it too would help to make us sing the glory of the Creator through the marvelous perfection of His work.[78]

But when he takes up on his own account, as a poet of our times, Francis Thompson, has done, the verse of *Psalm 25,2, Domine dilexi decorem domus tuae,*[79] the abstract beauty of the *numeri* is added to (not substituted for) the beauty of the body (*species*), beauty made, says he, of proportionate balance of parts, together with the brightness of color, *congruentia partium cum quadam coloris suauitate*.[80] And the admiration that we will feel for it will be the very same as the esthetic experience of the present life, with only this difference, that this contemplation of bodies will no longer trouble our souls by reason of the tumult of concupiscence. St. Augustine's attachment to this formal value of physical beauty is so strong that it dictates to him his reply to the famous objections drawn from the incomplete development of bodies, physical deformities, nails, or hair: there can no longer be anything ugly, disproportionate, discordant, anything which could offend the eye; everything will be possessed of perfect beauty in "those pure, youthful, eternally resplendent bodies."[81] And if anyone still wants to quibble about the identity of those henceforth flawless bodies with those which had been borne throughout life by their wretched owners, St. Augustine is not at a loss. He answers with the ingenious comparison, cited above, of the bronze statue which the artist sends back to the foundry so as to remodel it even more beautifully than before.[82]

Resplendent, yes, but recognizable, it will indeed remain always the same body with all its identifying marks, and first among them, sex. St. Augustine cuts short those rather turbid speculations according to which women would in the resurrection be changed to men, speculations deriving from Gnostic circles whose myths, as is well known, express so many obsessions that were sexual in origin. (Thus, for the Valentinians, at the time of the eschatological "gathering" of the "seeds," the Pneumatics take on a feminine form and unite as spouses with the Angels of the Savior.) [83] These ideas did not fail to spread to some of the boldest theologians such as Origen. Echoes of them are perceptible even in St. Jerome, whom it has been possible to charge with having held that at the resurrection *uxores in uiros conuertantur,*[84] and even among the faithful, as is evidenced in a curious passage of the *Martyrdom of SS. Perpetua and Felicitas.*[85] No, once again, nothing will be changed in the body except what was affected by corruptibility. Now, woman's sex is not a defect, but her nature, *non est autem vitium sexus femineus sed natura*; woman, as such, is a creature of God just as truly as man. Scrutinizing, as usual, the iota of the word of Scripture, St. Augustine calls attention to the famous passage concerning the woman married successively to seven brothers. The Gospel says specifically that there will be no marriage, but not that there will be no women at the resurrection. Better, in deliberately saying that then "neither will

26

men take wives, nor women husbands," the Lord shows clearly that there will be both men and women![86]

In heaven all will be as before the advent of sin: man and woman were naked and were not ashamed. Woman will be adorned with a new beauty which will no longer arouse desire (for that will no longer be), but which will evoke praise for the wisdom and the goodness of God who has made what was not, and has purified what He has made. Here I must in passing call attention to a remarkable similarity between this chapter of the *City of God* and the highest speculation of the East. In the admirable chapter which St. John Climacus has devoted to the virtue of purity, we read that any one who in contemplating the beauty of a human body would be led by that sight only to glorify the Creator in the *agapè* and in tears, would be already raised up, incorruptible, without having to await the general resurrection.[87]

Therefore this body which arises, freed henceforth from all corruption, is not an abstract principle of material being, but, in its concrete reality, the very same body. No lengthy pondering on the principle of individuality is needed in order to realize all that the certainty of having one's own body again adds to the security of survival of one's own person. This problem is a difficult and perhaps insoluble one in the perspective in which we earlier considered it with reference to Greek thought, wherein man is defined as soul or spirit in virtue of being an emanation of a divine substance. This difficulty, moreover, is not restricted to the philosophies of classical paganism. We need only advert to the philosophies of India which proclaim the identification of *Atman* and *Brahman!* Christian faith, on the other hand, gives us the assurance of being reunited to the former companion of our joys and sorrows, that body which has fought and suffered. Just as the risen Christ could show to the unbelieving Thomas the marks of the lance and the nails,[88] so, says St. Augustine, on the bodies of the martyrs their glorious scars will shine.[89] Together with this particular, or better, this particularized body, it is our own individuality, whole and entire, that is assured of survival. The individual that we were is, so to say, modeled and formed by our own history, and we can even say, will have become itself by means of that history. This idea, which has become familiar to modern man, was perhaps first realized by St. Augustine, as Paul Louis Landsberg has previously shown.[90] Who, prior to the author of the *Confessions,* had been able to show, as Augustine did, the development of a personality in the working of his interior evolution?

It is the whole of man, soul and body, that will live again. The *mutatio* which we were considering, while putting an end to corruptibility, leaves to each his own characteristics, especially the particular sentiments which animated him. St. Augustine draws from this certitude thoughts which he develops beautifully in his letters of condolence. Thus, to a grieving sister: "The love with which your brother loved you and loves you still has not died; it lives on, preserved in treasure and hidden with Christ in the Lord. . . ."[91] "We do not lose those who have gone before us out of this life; we send them on ahead, as it were, into that other life where we shall rejoin them and where they will be all the dearer to us for our knowing them more intimately": *ubi nobis erunt quanto notiores tanto utique chariores.*[92]

Here again St. Augustine appears as the precursor of modern personalism. Contemporary philosophy, attempting to analyze the role of reciprocity in consciousness, has given prominence to the essential bond between relationship and person which the theology of the Trinity had been the first to divine. To say that our individuality continues to exist is also to affirm the perdurance of the entire fabric, woven throughout the whole of our life by the complex of relationships established between our deepest self and God, between ourselves and our human brethren, and finally, between us and the world where we have acted, reacted, struggled, suffered, and created.

St. Augustine has particularly highlighted the necessary connection between the resurrection of the body (and therefore of the person) and the transfiguration of the cosmos. This point deserves attention because it is a theme which does not appear very often in his writings. It has been many times repeated, and rightly, that St. Augustine is not much interested in what might be called the cosmic component of salvation.[93] In his first writings, which were still too subservient to Neoplatonism, he ventured to sum up the whole program of a philosophy in the simple binomial: *de anima, de Deo.* He had no place, it seems, for a *peri kosmou.*[94] Nothing is more significant than to see him wrestling with the famous verses of *Romans* (8, 19-22), where a disciple of Fr. Teilhard de Chardin will always delight in recognizing the deep inspiration of his master:[95] "All creation groans and travails in pain until now . . . ." *Omnis creatura,* reads St. Augustine, and he understands it thus: Man, in whom the whole of creation is recapitulated [96]—man, not the cosmos.[97]

However, attentive exegete that he was, he could not neglect the formulae taken from Isaiah,[98] which the *Apocalypse* mentions concerning "a new heaven and a new earth."[99] And, theologian that he was, he could not fail to assign its place to the role of this cosmic component when, in bringing to a finish his great plan for the *City of God,* he had to sketch the treatise on the last things.[100] The final destiny of the world, and that of man, are intimately bound up with each other. The end of the world will also be, *mirabili mutatione,* a transfiguration rather than annihilation.[101] *Figura ergo praeterit, non natura:*[102] the face of the world will pass away, but not its substance— which, when purified by fire, will emerge in a better state. As with man, so with the cosmos: everything corruptible in it will be destroyed, but without its own substance disappearing. On the contrary, by means of that elimination it will acquire new qualities, in accord with those of risen man. For it is necessary that the universe also be renewed for the better, *in melius innouatus,* so as to be in harmony with the body of man which also will be renewed.[103]

Once again, together with the cosmic setting, it is man in his wholeness and his values that will be saved. Whether for cosmos or for man, eschatology appears as a consummation rather than a destruction. What will be destroyed at the *immutatio caelestis* is evil, that non-being; corruptibility, that aptitude to diminution, that exposure to nothingness. What disappears in this way is properly non-value. Everything in man—and let us repeat it unwearingly, in the whole man, body or flesh, soul and mind—everything that had positive reality, that shared in the category of good, *bona,* all of that, purified of any associated imperfection, enters into eternity, as silver purified in the crucible, as the good grain separated from the chaff, as the wheat from the tares.

From this viewpoint, eschatalogical transfiguration, far from impoverishing us, fills us to overflowing. True human values are not only preserved and maintained, they are thenceforth brought to the fullness of their reality. For indeed, while they were limited to our earthly experience, these values, whether esthetic delight, human love, or experience of things heavenly, are never lived more than in an inchoate and precarious state. This is the painful experience which the prophetic message of our poets has succeeded in recording, Hoelderlin among them:

It is only for brief moments that man can bear

31

the divine plenitude; life thereafter is no more than the dream of those moments.[104]

This is a truth which ancient wisdom had in its own way already glimpsed and expressed. St. Augustine devotes long passages to the variety of miseries that fill man's life[105]—a sinister picture which portrays, as in an etching or on a photographic negative, the pathetic longing for happiness which fills men's hearts. Present-day readers are sometimes surprised, not to say shocked, by the rhetorical tone of such chapters. It is true that St. Augustine is doing no more than developing a commonplace of the classic diatribe (theme no. 75 of the Oltramare catalog [106]), but this only means that Cynico-Stoic preaching from Teles to Seneca had already gazed sincerely and deeply into the sorrowful state of man in this terrestrial life. Why should St. Augustine hesitate to borrow from it this disillusioned and authentic likeness? Those philosophers had clearly seen that man was made for happiness and that he could not find it here below. This beatitude, this *beata uita,* which the whole Hellenistic philosophy had vainly striven to define and to pursue (recall the two hundred eighty-eight definitions of the sovereign good according to Varro which St. Augustine ironically inventories at the beginning of Book XIX of his *City of God*)—God will give this beatitude to the risen saints in their immortal and spiritualized bodies.[107]

But if it is possible to risk sketching a conjectural picture of what such *felicitas* will be, [108] this can only

32

be done by extrapolation from the good things which God has already allowed us to taste during this earthly life. For true values were just that: good things. We saw it in the case of physical beauty; all the more so is it true of moral beauty. In the physical order as in the moral, harmony and peace will then reign—that *pax* which St. Augustine has magnificently praised in the first book of the *City of God* (ch. 19) —peace within ourselves, peace in our relationships with others. (For life in the heavenly city is a social life.[109] Nothing could be more foreign to the Augustinian concept than to imagine each soul bound, so to say, exclusively, by direct line to God, and leaving others out of account. We must not forget that we are and shall remain members one of another, forming the same body, that of Christ in his plenitude.) And finally, peace towards God.[110]

And in this reconciliation of all things, we shall be able to exercise in all its fulness our freedom, our true freedom, that to which all sanctity, which glimpses it as far as possible, never ceases to aspire. No longer that freedom, so dearly bought, to keep from sinning, but that by which we shall share in the divine freedom, the freedom from being even able to sin.[111] Free as regards evil, we shall be unfettered, no longer consumed by difficult or useless occupations—free, but active. Indolence or boredom will be no more.[112] Exercise, activity, interest in work must therefore be good things in themselves. Occupied, but with what, if not with love, the vision of God (whether in the body or out of the body, God knows)[113] with contemplation, and with praise?[114] St. Augustine likes to call this eternal life the great sabbath, *maximum sabbatum;* [115] but let us hasten to add that this image evokes for him above all the idea of consecrated time ("where we shall be filled with His blessing and His sanctification") rather than the idea of repose in the sense in which in the Latin vocabulary *otium* is opposed to activity (*neg-otium*). This must be emphasized, because some persons, in order the better to exalt the dynamic conception which such of the Greek Fathers as Gregory of Nyssa have of eternal life,[116] are too much inclined to depreciate St. Augustine, as if he offered us a theology for weary and decadent intellectuals aspiring to be unburdened of labor and effort and aiming only at repose.

Yes, it is quite true that from the pen of St. Augustine there come thronging images that are more or less taken up with the end of life, so as to call forth this eschatalogical realization of human destiny. It will be the *Amen,*[117] the eternal yes, the Alleluia,[118], the Dedication,[119] the crowning of the eternal Church. But once again this ultimate stage is an active stage; repose, indeed, but not emptiness, repose in comparison with the terrestrial servitudes that were so overwhelming, but filled with that activity which is contemplation, love, praise. It is with a sorites composed on these themes that the last book of the *City of God* comes to its close.[120]

This brings us to a somewhat liturgical concept of eternal life. We shall join the choirs of Angels, our fellow-citizens in the City of God,[121] filling and, perhaps, more than filling the empty places left by the defection of the wicked Angels.[122] Here as elsewhere, in trying to express the fulness of his religious thought and all the lyricism of his Christian heart, St. Augustine effaces himself behind the inspired verses of Holy Scripture: "Happy they who dwell in your house! Continually they praise you. . . ." "The favors of the Lord I will sing forever."[123]

Having reached this point, the theology of St. Augustine utters a final challenge to the modern conscience, which, as we have mentioned, is so anxious to recover and to ensure its cherished human values. It forces us to ask the question: What are these values? What are the true human values? From Augustine's viewpoint the answer is easy, but its practical consequences are limitless. As always with the Fathers, and as in all true theology, theory is oriented to *praxis,* and speculation flowers in spirituality. The true human values are those spiritual values at which we have finally arrived: contemplation, praise, love. If man is truly that creature fashioned for God, capable of God, when will he most fully attain his being, when is he most truly human, if not when he even now orients his life—his earthly life, that is, his most present one—towards this ideal of consecrated and liturgical life, which true life, heavenly life will be?

"He who would save his life will lose it." We

should grasp the full import of this solemn warning of the Gospel whose form, paradoxical and challenging as it is, all too often tends to veil its urgency. It is not by clinging desperately to what is ephemeral, passing, declining, that man can satisfy the deepest demands of his nature. What count for him, or ought to, are the values which even here below anticipate eternity. Now those values are intimately woven into daily experience. In her most recent volume of memoirs, Simone de Beauvoir tries to attain a kind of stoic serenity, now that maturity and the weight of life bring her face to face with the problem of aging and of death. When she reaches the last page, she admirably evokes the "human values" which her life, so intensely lived, had known: "I think with melancholy of all the books read, the places visited, the knowledge acquired, which will no longer exist. All the music, all the painting, all the culture, so many places: suddenly, nothing. . . ." Here she once lets the word escape—as the word *anastasis* also once came from the pen of Plotinus—the word which sums up all the Christian hope: that of resurrection. The recalling of scenes or splendid landscapes which she has lived or contemplated closes with these words: ". . . the copper beach, the sleepless nights of Leningrad, the bells of Liberation, an orange moon over Piraeus, the red sun rising over the desert, Torcello, Rome, all the things I have spoken of, others of which I have said nothing—nothing of all that will rise again. . . ."[124] It may be that the word slipped out by accident; yet what meaning this technical word of our theology comes to have in this context!

Nothing of all that will rise again? It would be true if this landscape had served as setting for some unforgivable flood of passion; if those episodes of the past were linked to the effervescence of our pride, greed, untruthfulness, sin. But each time that this landscape, because it was beautiful and our heart opened up to new-found happiness in it, has been for the sanctified soul the occasion of a sacrifice of praise; and each time this music served, not to nourish concupiscence, but by silencing the tumult of thoughts and imaginations to re-establish in us the interior silence which permits the expectation of and the meeting with God; similarly, each time for every really deep esthetic experience; so too, for every human love—then, on the contrary, nothing of all this will be lost.

The most human life, the richest in values, is not that of the wretched sinner abandoned to the web of his falls, but rather the holiest life, the most spiritual—an essentially ascetic life, since inevitably *cette maison nous allons la quitter*,[125] but one, which, even here, opens out to contemplation and praise, an anticipation of that day which will have no end. Enlightened by all that has preceded, we can now take up again that scriptural verse which seemed at the outset to pose a problem for us. Yes, it is true, literally true: "Seek first,"—seek *now* and in everything—"the kingdom of God and his justice, and all these things"— all these values—"shall be given you besides."

On this level all schools of spirituality meet. Recourse to St. Augustine does not enclose us in a dark and exclusive "Latinism." In closing I must emphasize this point, particularly in the ecumenical period through which the Church is now passing, namely, that the wisdom which St. Augustine teaches us does not differ greatly from that of the great spiritual writers of the Eastern Church. (What reader of the *Confessions* could forget the role which the finding of the *Life of St. Anthony,* the first of the desert fathers, played for St. Augustine at a decisive moment on the eve of his conversion?) Was not the whole of Eastern monasticism itself oriented to the *bios isangelicos,* anticipation and first fruits of the *immutatio angelica?*

NOTES

1. *De la Connaissance historique*, Paris[4] 1964, p. 186.

2. *Soliloquia,* I, 1 (2-3), and especially: Deus universitatis conditor . . . Deus quem amat omne quod potest amare, siue sciens, siue nesciens . . . Te inuoco, Deus ueritas, in quo et a quo et per quem uera sunt quae sunt omnia, Deus sapientia . . . Deus uera et summa uita . . . Deus beatitudo . . . .

3. *Matthew* 6, 33 quoted by St. Augustine in: *De serm. Dom. in monte* II, 7 (25); *Serm.* 58, 4 (5); *Serm.* 57, 13 (13); *Conf.* XI, 2 (4); *Enarr. in Ps.* 143, 18; *Tract. in Job.* 122, 4.

4. See especially *Serm.* 103 and 104; for the rest, F. Cayré, *La contemplation augustinienne,* Paris[2] 1954, p. 42-48.

5. *Epist. ad. episcopos Galliarum,* 2.

6. *De fide et symb.* 6 (13); 10 (23-24).

7. *Opus imperf. c. Iulianum* VI, 31-40.

8. *Enchiridion* 23 (84-93).

9. He uses in turn three different words to indicate the Creed: 1) *Confessio fidei*: *Epist. ad. Rom. quar. prop. expos.* 67; *C. Faustum* XII, 26; *Epist.* 187, 3 (10). 2) *Symbolum*: *Serm.* 214, 1; *Serm.* 213, 1; *De Fide et symb.* 1 (1), 10 (25); *Enchir.* 2 (7); *De Symbolo,* 1 (1). 3) *Regula fidei*: *Sermo* 213, 1; *De Symbolo,* 1 (1) *Retract.* II, 3.

10. It is noteworthy that the theme of the resurrection of the body occurs three times in this small work: 7 (11), a general program of "pre-catechesis"; 25 (46), a model of an elaborate presentation; 27 (54), a model of a briefer presentation.

11. For example, *Sermo Guelferb.* 1, 10 (a text which is preferable to that of *Serm. Maur.* 213, (9); *Serm.* (*Maur.*) 214, 12; *De symbolo ad catechumenos* 1, 9 (17).

12. Here one may, with qualifications, make use of a concept which, as we know, has only been brought out by modern historians, beginning with J. Daillé, *Traité de l'employ des saints Pères,* Genève, 1632, p. 170-174.

13. See the Maurists' note to the title of *Serm.* 212, *P. L.* 38, 1058 (*b*); the title *Dominica in ramis Palmarum* is more recent and was not in use at Hippo in St. Augustine's day. The Saturday before the fourth Sunday of Lent has also been suggested. See the discussions by B. Busch, *Ephem. Liturg.* 52 (1938), p. 440-446; P. Verbracken, *Rev. Bénéd.* 68 (1958), p. 5. *Adhuc sub iudice lis est.*

14. *Serm.* 336-338.

15. *Enarr. in Ps.* 29, *serm.* 1-2.

16. The *fides Christianorum,* the specific and the fundamental belief of Christians, which distinguishes them from pagans and Jews, is faith in the resurrection of Christ. This statement made by Augustine, often in connection with the Pauline verse *Rom.* 10, 9, recurs in

Contra Faustum XVI, 29; *Epist.* 55, 2; *Serm.* 234, 3; *De Trinit.* II, 17 (29); *Enarr. in Ps.* 101, *s.* 2, 7; *in Ps.* 120, 6; *Serm. Denis,* 24, 1; (*Maur.*) 233, 1 (1); 215, 6; 240, 2; 241, 1; *Enarr. in Ps.* 138, 8.

17. The four accounts of Christ's resurrection according to the four Evangelists were read successively during the course of the week *in albis.* These *lectiones certae* furnished St. Augustine with the occasion for some commentaries. These include, mainly, the sermons of *Luke* which have come down to us (the pericope of the disciples of Emmaus), which were preached on either Tuesday or Wednesday of Easter Week, and the sermons on *John* (*Noli me tangere,* the second miraculous draught of fish, the triple confession of St. Peter), preached on Thursday, Friday, and Saturday.

18. By His resurrection, Christ has given the members of the Body, whose Head He is, the *exemplum* of the *resurrectio carnis*: *Contra Faustum* XI, 3; *Contra Felicem* II, 11; *Enarr. in Ps.* 101, *s.* 2, 14; *in Ps.* 56, 1-2; *De Trinitate* IV, 3 (6), 6 (10); *Enarr. in Ps.* 55, 3; *Serm.* 240, 2 (2); 241, 1 (1); *Enarr. in Ps.* 70, *s.* 2, 10; *in Ps.* 34, *s.* 2, 3; *Epist.* 205, 8; *Serm.* 361, 10 (10).

19. Not that he refrains from commenting on it in its entirety. Certain verses, as we shall see, are frequently used; others are passed over almost in silence. Thus *I. Cor.,* 15, 12 is used in a resurrection context only in two passages: *Contra Faustum* XI, 3; *Ad Donatist. post collationem* 21 (34).

20. The Manicheans invoked especially verse *I. Cor.* 15, 50 (". . . flesh and blood can obtain no part in the kingdom of God"). This is why St. Augustine often returned to this text. We find it quoted no less than twenty-five times, either in commentaries on the articles of the Creed: *De fide et symbolo* 10 (24); *De agone christiano* 32 (34); *De doctrina christiana I,* 19 (18); *Enchiridion* 23 (91); *Sermo* 362, 13, 18; or in a refutation of the

Manichean interpretation of this verse: *Contra Fortunatum* 19; *De fide et symb., loc. cit., Contra Adimantum* 12 (1, 4, 5); *De agone christ., loc. cit.; Contra Faustum* XI, 3, 7; XVI, 29; XXII, 17; v. also *Contra adv. leg. et proph.* II, 6 (22); *Epist.* 205, 2 (5, 13-16); *Retract.* I, 17; II, 3. St. Augustine's principal argument is furnished by the verse *Luke* 24, 39: "See my hands and feet . . . ." (Thus: *De Trinit.* IV, 3, 6).

21. Cf. *Recherches Augustiniennes*, I, Paris 1958, p. 149-186.

22. See my article "La Résurrection des morts et les Apologistes," in *Lumière et Vie*, 3 (1952), p. 83-92.

23. Cf. C. Lambot. *Rev. Bénéd.* 57 (1947), p. 89-108, and especially pp. 102-104, on the series of sermons of Easter Week (from Easter Day to the Sunday of the octave included), those of the "collection *Alleluia*" (*Serm.* 119, 240-243, 251, 147, 148 and 260). Sermons 240-243, which were preached Monday to Thursday, are given over to refuting the objections which the *philosophi* raised against the Resurrection.

Again, the feast of the Ascension and the commentary on *John* 3, 13 ("And no one has ascended into heaven except Him who has descended from heaven") led St. Augustine to refute the objection that the weight of the body rendered impossible Christ's being raised aloft; cf. *De agone christ.* 25 (27); *Serm. Mai* 98, 1-3; *Serm.* (*Maur.*) 263, 2-3; *Serm. Bibl. Casin.* II, 76 (2).

24. To the texts already cited, there could be added (without at all exhausting the list) such examples as: *Serm.* 242, 3 (5); *De civ. Dei* XIII, 18.

25. *De civ. Dei* XXII, 4 (quoting Cicero, *De Republ.* III, fr. 40); cf. XXII, 6, 1.

26. *De civ. Dei* XXII, 20, 4.

27. *Enchiridion* 23 (89); *De civ. Dei* XX, 19, 1.

28. *Hom. in Matth.* 34, 4, *P. G.* 57, c. 403.

29. Porphyry, *Vit. Plot.* 1, p. 1, 1.1-2 Henry-Schwyzer.

30. *De civ. Dei* XIV, 3, 2, quoting *Aeneid* VI, 730 (the family motto of Teilhard de Chardin)—733.

31. First in an anti-Manichean perspective: *Contra Faustum* XX, 22; *Enarr. in Ps.* 141, 18-19. Later on it seems to have been Origen's teaching which he had in mind: *Serm.* 277, 3; *Epist.* 166, 5 (15), 9 (27); 164, 7 (20).

32. *Enneads* III, 6, 6, p. 345-346, 1. 86-77. Ed. Henry-Schwyzer.

33. *Vit. Plot.* 3, p. 3; 25-27 H.-Schw. I have translated the commonly accepted text; P. Henry, "La dernière parole de Plotin," *Studi Classici e Orientali* (Pisa) II (1953), p. 113-130, gives a different reading of the text: "Endeavor to raise up the God within you even to the Divine which is in the universe."

34. *De Ressurectione* (*Epistula ad Rheginum*). *Codex Jung f. XXIIr-f. XXVv* (p. 43-50), ed. M. Malinine *et al.*, Zürich-Stuttgart 1963, p. 45, 24-49, 30 and the note by H. Ch. Puech *ad* 47, 2-8 (p. 34).

35. St. Augustine has several times commented on *II. Tim.* 2, 18; *Contra Faustum* IV, 2; *De baptismo* III, 19 (26); IV, 12 (18); *Epist.* 55, 3 (4); *Serm.* 362, 19 (22); *Enarr. in Ps.* 92, 5: *Tract. in Joh. ev.* 19, 14; 22, 11-12.

36. Origen, *Contra Celsum* VII, 33-36; VIII, 49.

37. *De civ. Dei* X, 29, 2; XIII, 19; XXII, 12, 26-28; *Retract.* I, 4 (4).

38. *Serm.* 241, 7.

39. John J. O'Meara, *Porphyry's Philosophy from Oracles in Augustine,* Paris 1959, *pass.* (v. p. 183A s.v. *omne corpus fugiendum*).

43

40. St. Augustine will say, "participate in God": *De civ. Dei* XXII, 30, 3: "Aliud est enim esse Deum, aliud participem Dei. Deus natura peccare non potest, particeps uero Dei ab illo accepit ut peccare non possit."

41. St. Augustine frequently attacks this Manichean error: *Conf.* XIII, 30 (45); *Contra Faustum* XX, 15, 22; *Enarr. in Ps.* 141, 18; *Serm. Morin* 10, 3; *Serm. (Maur.)* 154, 9 (13).

42. The text from *Genesis*, 1. 31 ("et uidit Deus omnia quae fecit et ecce bona ualde"), was dear to St. Augustine (he quoted it nearly fifty times). He makes use of it especially to prove the value which the human body holds in God's creative plan: *De diu. quaest.* 83, qu. 10 and 51; *De Gen. ed litt. lib. imperf.* 16 (59); *Conf.* XIII, 38 (43); *De Gen. ad. litt.* III, 24 (36); *Enarr. in Ps.* 145, 3; *De civ. Dei* XI, 23, 1; *Contra Iulian.* VI, 7 (20).

43. See the allusion to Apollinarism in a context relating to the dual resurrection: ("corpus ex infirmitate, anima ex iniquitate"): *Tract. in Joh. ev.* 23, 6.

44. *De Trinitate* II, 17 (29).

45. This is not so different from St. Augustine's own terminology, *De civ. Dei* XIII, 24, 2: "homo et anima constat et corpore."

46. *De civ. Dei* XIV, 3, 2: "nec caro corruptibilis animam peccatricem, sed anima peccatrix fecit esse corruptibilem carnem"; XIV, 13, 1, commenting on *Sirach* 10, 15, "The origin of every sin is pride."

47. *De catechiz. rudibus* 7 (11): corporis resurrectio; 27 (54); resurrectio mortuorum; resurrectionem . . . caro . . . .

48. This table, constructed with reference only to *De fide et symb.* may be misleading. The reader should understand that the table, even though complex, does not

exhaust all the variations which St. Augustine made on this same theme. Elsewhere, for example in *Serm.* 214, 12, man is analyzed as *anima* and *caro;* and again, in *Epist.* 263, 4, as *mens* and *caro* (in both cases, *caro* means simply "the body").

49. *De civ. Dei* XXII, 29, 4.

50. *De civ. Dei* XXII, 21: (Deo) ipso adiuuante, coniciamus, ut possumus, quantum sit illius quod nondum experti utique digne eloqui non ualemus . . . .

51. *Enchiridion* 23 (91); *Serm.* 242, 8 (11); 277, 4 (4).

52. See again the texts assembled above in note 16.

53. *De symbolo ad catechumenos, serm.* 1 (this alone is authentic), 9 (17).

54. *Contra Faustum* XI, 7; *Epist.* 205, 2 (8).

55. *De civ. Dei* XXII, 14.

56. *Contra Faustum* XI, 3; cf. *Serm. Guelferb.* 1, 4.

57. *Serm.* 362, 15 (18); *De civ. Dei* XXII, 17.

58. *Mutatio: Serm.* 362, 16 (19); *M. caelestis: Contra Adimantum* 12, 4. *Commutatio caelestis incorruptionis: De catech. rud.* 23 (46); *C. angelica:* Id. 27 (54). *Immutatio: C. Adim.* 12, 4-5; *Serm.* 362, 18 (21); *Imm. angelica: De fide et symb.* 10 (24).

59. In the *De agone christiano* 32 (34), with reference to the same controverted verse, *I. Cor.* 15, 50 ("flesh and blood can obtain no part in the kingdom of God"), St. Augustine had written that after the resurrection "iam non erit caro et sanguis; sed caeleste corpus." He now says more exactly: "non sic accipiendum est quasi carnis non sit futura substantia, sed carnis et sanguinis nomine ipsam corruptionem carnis et sanguinis intelligendus est Apostolus nuncupasse . . . ," *Retract.* II, 4 (3).

Similarly, in *Retract.* I, 17, apropos of *De fide*: it is the very same body that will be restored to us, recognizable as was that of the risen Christ.

60. *Epist.* 205, 2 (11), and previously 1 (4), 2 (14); the theme constantly recurs. See especially *Serm.* 362, 16 (19) and also *Tract. in Joh.* ev. 20, 5 (12); *Enarr. in Ps.* 50, 19; *in Ps.* 102, 6; *Enchiridion* 23 (91-92); *De civ. Dei* XX, 6, 2.

61. As in *Serm.* 362, 15 (17)—18 (21); *Serm.* 242, 3 (4).

62. *De civ. Dei* XIII, 16, 1. St. Augustine often returned to *Wisdom* 6, 15, as in: *Enarr. in Ps.* 127, 16; 84, 10; 102, 6; 50, 19; 62, 6-7; *De Trinit.* IV, 3 (5) . . . .

63. *De civ. Dei,* 13, 19.

64. *De civ. Dei XIII,* 16-17; XXII, 26-28.

65. For the body it will be complete healing, "sanitas perfecta": *Enarr. in Ps.* 63, 9; *Serm. Guelferb.* 33, 2; *Enarr. in Ps.* 122, 12; 146, 6; 29, s. 2, 12; 102, 5; 55, 6; *Serm.* 278, 5 (5); the return to the *pristina stabilitas,* as it was prior to original sin: *De uera religione* 12 (25), 23 (44); *Retract.* I, 13, 4.

66. *Serm.* 362, 16 (19); *De civ. Dei* XIII, 23, 1.

67. G. B. Ladner, *The Idea of Reform, its Impact on Christian Thought and Action in the Age of the Fathers,* Cambridge (Mass.) 1959; see my recension in *Revue d'Histoire Ecclésiastique,* 1962, 139-141.

68. *De fide et symb.* 10 (23).

69. *Contra Faustum* XVI, 29.

70. As in the *De civ. Dei* XIV, 11, 1.

71. See the excellent documentation compiled by A. Orbe in *Estudios Valentinianos. 2. En los álbores de la*

exegesis johannea (*Analecta Gregoriana* 65), Roma 1955, 275-319.

72. *De civ. Dei* XIII, 10; the theme almost becomes an obsession; *Enarr. in Ps.* 38, 3-12; *in Ps.* 62, 6-7; *in Ps.* 128, 15; *De Trinit.* IV, 3 (5).

73. *De civ. Dei* XXII, 1, 1.

74. *De div. quaest.* 83, qu. 11; 51; *De Gen. ad. litt. lib. imperf.* 16 (59); *Enarr. in Ps.* 32, II. s. 2, 21; *De Continentia* 10 (24); *Serm.* 241, 7 (7); 243, 3 (3)—(4); 362, 15 (18); *De civ. Dei* XXII, 17; 19, 2; 20, 3.

75. Recall in this connection the very pertinent comments of Fr. Chatillon, *Hic, ibi, interim,* in *Melangés Marcel Viller* (*Revue d'Ascétique et de Mystique* 1949), 194-199.

76. *Serm.* 243, 8 (7), *P.L.* 38, c. 1146-1147: Sic ergo, carissimi, sic credite, sic tenete, multorum membrorum ibi usum non futurum, sed decus nullius defuturum. Nihil indecorum erit ibi, summa pax erit, nihil discordans, nihil monstruosum, nihil quod offendat adspectum, in omnibus Deus laudabitur. Nam si nunc in ista infirmitate carnis et tenera operatione membrorum apparet tanta corporis pulchritudo, quae illicit libidinosos, et ad quaerendum excitat siue studiosos siue curiosos, et si inueniatur in corpore ratio numerorum, non alius artifex horum, alius inuenitur esse coelorum, sed idem ipse creator infimorum atque summorum; quanto magis ibi, ubi erit libido nulla, nulla corruptio, nulla deformis prauitas, nulla aerumnosa necessitas, sed interminata aeternitas, pulchra ueritas, summa felicitas?

77. *De Musica* VI, 45 (49); *De Trinit.* IV, 3 (5-6); *De civ. Dei* XXII, 24, 4.

78. *De civ. Dei* XXII, 30, 1.

79. *De civ. Dei* XXII, 21.

80. *Epist.* 3, 4. Concerning this definition, which derived from Stoic influence, and was developed beginning with Cicero, *Disputiones Tusculanae* IV, 30-31; cf. K. Svoboda, *L' esthétique de saint Augustin et ses sources,* Brno 1933, p. 54; cf. *De musica,* VI, 13 (38).

81. To echo the words of a moving Lied by Oliver Messiaen, *Poèmes pour Mi,* 1er Livre, 3. *La maison* (1937).

82. See the texts cited above, n. 27.

83. St. Irenaeus, I, 1, 14, p. 15 Harvey; Clement of Alexandria, *Extraits de Theodotus,* 64, p. 186 Sagnard.

84. Rufinus, *Apologia* I, 25, criticizing the *Commentary* of Jerome on *Eph.* 5, 28-29, *P.L.* 26, c. 534B; cf. *Adu. Iovinianum* I, 16, *P.L.* 23, c. 235C. In his rejoinder, *Apologia adu. lib. Rufini, P.L.* 23, c. 414 BD, Jerome throws the blame on his Greek sources and especially on Origen (whose commentary on *Ephesians* has been lost).

85. *Passio SS. Perpetuae et Felicitatis,* 10, 7: . . . *et expoliata sum et facta sum masculus.*

86. *De civ. Dei* XXII, 17.

87. St. John Climacus, *Scala Parad.* 15, 60, P.G. 188, c. 891D-893A.

88. *Serm.* 242, 2 (3); cf. *Epist.* 205, 2 (9-10).

89. *De civ. Dei* XXII, 19, 3.

90. A French edition of his scattered various and un-published writings on St. Augustine is being prepared by the Editions du Seuil.

91. *Epist.* 263, 2: neque enim . . . periit illa charitas qua Timotheus Sapidam dilexit et diligit: manet illa seru-ata in thesauro suo et abscondita est cum Christo in Domino.

92. *Epist.* 92, 1.

93. Th. E. Clarke, *The eschatological Transformation of the material World according to saint Augustine,* Woodstock 1956 (ch. 6, "The Groaning of Creation," from an unpublished thesis of the Gregorian University); from the same: "St. Augustine and Cosmic Redemption," *Theological Studies,* 19 (1958), 133-164.

94. To use again the expression which I employed in *Saint Augustin et la fin de la culture antique,* Paris[4] 1958, p. 233. It is of course true that, reaching for the transcendent, as he does, he will always seek to pass beyond the cosmos. For example, the *Tract. in Joh. e.v.* 20, 13, ends with the same ardent impulse as the "ecstasy" of Ostia.

95. Permit me in this connection to refer to a work written in my youth: *Fondements d'une culture chrétienne,* Paris 1934, 110-113.

96. *De. diu. quaest.* 83, qu. 67, 5.

97. This same interpretation is found from *De fide et symb.* 10 (23) to *Contra Priscill. et Origen.* 8 (11). Always a careful exegete, attentive to context, St. Augustine is at pains to specify that by the *creatura* of v. 22, are meant men who are as yet unbelievers, as opposed to the faithful, who are designated as "sons" or "children of God" in vv. 19 and 21: *Expos. Ep. ad. Gal.* 63; *Enarr. in Ps.* 125, 2; 118, s. 12, 1.

This anti-cosmic exegesis, which St. Ephrem alone among the Fathers shares with him, is explained in St. Augustine's case by the anti-Manichean controversy: he is unwilling to extend the meaning of *creatura* to the material universe for fear that someone might think he meant, as the Manicheans did, that trees or stones could lament: *Quaedam propos. ex. Ep. de Rom. expos.* 53.

98. *Isaiah* 65, 17-19; 66, 22.

99. *Apoc.* 21, 1; cf. *II, Peter* 3, 13.

100. *De civ. Dei* XX, 14-18. The same theme is touched upon briefly in: *De uera relig.* 23 (44); *Conf.* VII, 21 (27); *De doctr. christ.* III, 34 (49); *Retract.* 1, 3, 2; 4, 2; *De haeres.* 67.

101. *De civ. Dei* XX, 16.

102. *Id.* XX, 14.

103. *Id.* XXII, 29, 6.

104. In the elegy *Brot und Wein,* 114-115:
Nur zu Zeiten erträgt göttliche Fülle der Mensch.
Traum von ihnen ist darauf das Leben.

105. *De civ. Dei XXII,* 23-24; *Serm.* 241, 4 (4).

106. A. Oltramare, *Les origines de la diatribe romaine,* Genève 1926.

107. *De civ. Dei* XXII, 29.

108. *Id.* XXII, 21, 30.

109. *Id.* XIX, 5.

110. *Id.* XIX, 10-11; 13. St. Augustine links the personal happiness of each risen individual to the universal beatitude of the whole Church. He expresses it by the simile of a *holocaust* (perfect completion, purification by fire, total oblation to God): *Quaest. in Heptat.* VII, 49, 25; *De diu. quaest.* 83, qu. 67, 6; *Enarr. in Ps.* 65, 18, 20; 64, 4; 50, 23.

111. *De civ. Dei* XXII, 30, 3.

112. *De catech. rud.* 25 (47); cf. *Serm.* 255, 7 (7).

113. *De civ. Dei.* XXII, 29, 1-6.

114. *Id.* XXII, 30; 1.

115. *Id*. XXII, 30, 4; v. also XI, 8; *Conf*. XIII, 35 (50)—36 (51); *Enarr. in Ps*. 92, 1; *De Gen. ad. litt*. IV, 14 (25); *Serm*. 270, 5.

116. Cf. H. Urs. von Balthasar, in *Présence et Pensée, essai sur la philosophie religieuse de Grégoire de Nysse*, Paris 1942, p. 123-132, "Transposition du Devenir": "C'est le mystère de la *Présence* qui n'a jamais fini de venir . . . ."

117. *Serm*. 362, 28 (29): "Tota actio nostra Amen et Alleluia erit."

118. *Serm*. 243, 9 (8).

119. *De civ. Dei* XV, 19 and the three *Sermons*. 336–338 *in dedicatione eeclesiae*.

120. *De civ. Dei* XXII, 30: *Ibi uacabimus et uidebimus; uidebimus et amabimus; amabimus et laudabimus: ecce quod erit sine fine*.

121. *Id*. XII, 9, 2.

122. *Enchiridion* 9 (29); *De civ. Dei* XXII, 1, 2. It is the analogy of a choir, diversified but harmonious, which helps most towards understanding the unequal degrees of excellence among the elect: cf. *Enchir*. 23 (90).

123. *Ps*. 83, 5 and 88, 1, quoted in the final chapter of the *De civ. Dei* XXII, 30.

124. S. de Beauvoir, *La force des choses*, Paris 1963, p. 686.

125. To quote once again the Lied of Olivier Messiaen.

THE SAINT AUGUSTINE LECTURES
VILLANOVA UNIVERSITY
VILLANOVA, PA.

1959   *Saint Augustine on Personality,* by Paul Henry, S.J., Institut Catholique, Paris, New York, The Macmillan Company, 1960.

1960   *Platonism and Augustinianism,* by Raymond Klibansky, McGill University, unpublished.

1961   *Charter of Christendom: the Significance of The City of God,* by John O'Meara, University College, Dublin, New York, The Macmillan Company, 1961.

1962   *At the Origins of the Thomistic Notion of Man,* by Anton Pegis, Pontifical Institute of Mediaeval Studies, Toronto, New York, The Macmillan Company, 1963.

1963   *Augustine's View of Reality,* by Vernon J. Bourke, St. Louis University, Villanova, Villanova Press, 1964.

1964   *Augustine and the Greek Philosophers,* by John F. Callahan, Georgetown University, Villanova, Villanova Press, 1967.

1966   *Saint Augustine and Christian Platonism,* by A. Hilary Armstrong, University of Liverpool, Villanova, Villanova Press, 1967.